Valley Forge:

The Birthplace of the US Army
US History 9th Grade
Children's American History

BABY PROFESSOR

EDUCATION KIDS

The American Continental Army camped at Valley Forge during the 1777-1778 winter. It was here that our forces became a true fighting unit under the direction of George Washington. It is often referred to as the birthplace of American Army.

Where is it located?

It is located in the southeastern corner of Pennsylvania approximately 25 miles northwest of Philadelphia.

Why did they
choose to
camp there?

George Washington decided to make their winter camp here for many reasons. It was near Philadelphia and the British made camp their winter camp there. He could watch them and protect Pennsylvania.

It was also far enough away from them that would allow him plenty of time if they attacked. The areas in Mount Misery and Mount Joy were good places to make fortifications if they were attacked since they were high. To the north, Schuylkill River also served as a barricade.

Who were our
leaders?

It was here that the Army became a fight force to be reckoned with. The three leaders that played a major role in forming this army were General George Washington, General Friedrich von Steuben, and General Marquis de Lafayette.

The commander-in-chief was George Washington during the Revolution. His guidance played a major role making it possible for the United States to gain independence.

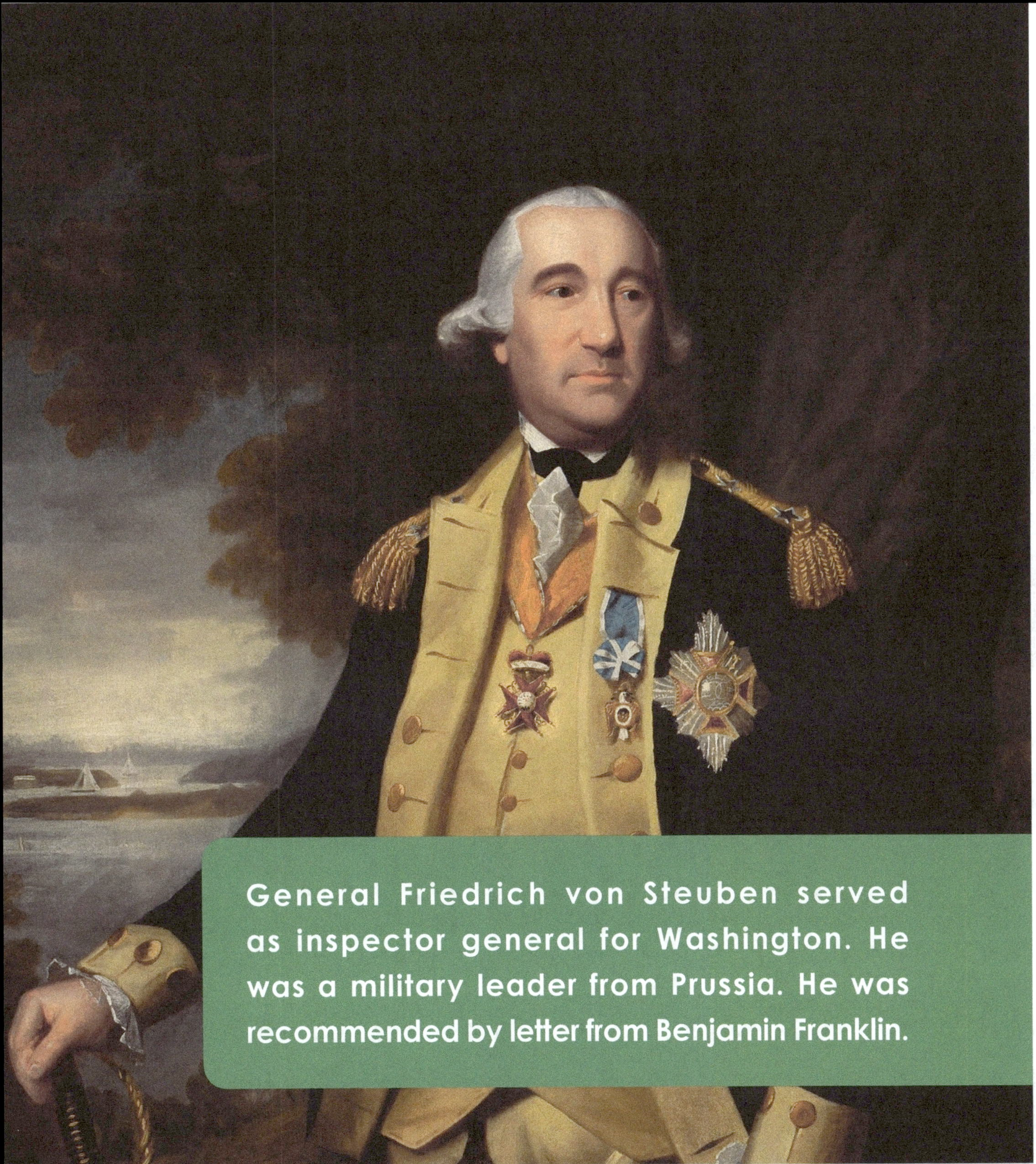
General Friedrich von Steuben served as inspector general for Washington. He was a military leader from Prussia. He was recommended by letter from Benjamin Franklin.

He trained the Army through his daily drills, even through the bitter cold. He taught disipline and fighting tactics to the soldiers.

He authored the Revolutionary War
Drill Manual which was used by US
forces until the War of 1812.

General de Lafayette was a leader of the French military who became a part of Washington's staff. He did not ask for special treatment or quarters, and did not receive any pay. He later became a significant commander at several major battles.

Conditions

The soldiers endured dire conditions at Valley Forge. It was snowy, wet, and cold. Food was scarce so they often were hungry.

Many of them didn't have clothing for warmth or shoes since their shoes would wear out on the long marches.

Blankets were hard to find as well. Living in log cabins that were crowded, damp, and cold made things worse allowing illness and disease to quickly spread throughout.

Smallpox, pneumonia and fever took the lives of many of the soldiers. Starting with 10,000 men in the winter, approximately 2,500 more passed away before arrival of spring.

Washington's sparsely fed and ill-equipped army stumbled into Valley Forge On December 19, 1777, fatigued from their extensive marches. Winds would blow as they prepared for the furry of winter.

Only approximately one-fourth of the soldiers had shoes to wear, leaving their bloody footprints. Grounds were then selected for the encampments, and the lines of defense began.

The first hut was constructed in three days. One hut would require 80 logs, and they had to walk for miles to collect the timber. Using only one axe, it was up in one week.

They provided the amount of protection needed from the typical wet and cold conditions during the winters in Pennsylvania.

Completion of the 2,000 huts was finished by the
beginning of February. While they did little to offset
the other shortages, they did provide shelter.

Washington demanded that each hut should have two windows by the spring as the weather became warmer. Mud also was chipped into the logs to make better ventilation.

Supplies and Food

Bread and meat were in short supply, and they would only be able to get nourishment from a tasteless mix of water and flour called "firecake." On occasion, they would have tripe broth flavored with pepper called pepper pot soup.

Snow was available only in small amounts and most of the time was not enough to be collected and melted for drinking water. Alternating the freezing and melting of it made it difficult to keep dry and disease would then fester.
MESS CHEST D.A.J.

Animals did not do much better. General Knox, the
Chief of Artillery, penned that hundreds of horses
either died of exhaustion or were starved to death.

Nathanael Greene was then appointed by Washington as Quartermaster General and he took charge of supplies.

In doing this, Washington advised that the situation with supplies was more dangerous to the survival of the army than Howe's army. Greene then found clothing and food and had them delivered for the horses and troops.

Clothing was also totally inadequate. Soldiers that had been wounded in earlier battles died due to exposure. The lengthy marches had destroyed their shoes.

Blankets were hard to come by. Garments that had been tattered were not usually replaced. These shortages then caused almost 4,000 soldiers to be listed unfit for duty.

Hardships

They were poorly clothed and undernourished, lived in damp, crowded quarters, and succumbed to disease and sickness. Among the numerous illnesses, typhoid, typhus, smallpox, dysentery, and pneumonia thrived in their camp during winter.

They contributed to some 2,500 men by winter's end, with exposure to the freezing temperatures and malnutrition also contributing to the deaths.

As hardships became more than they could tolerate, soldiers bean deserting in astonishing numbers. General Varnum warned that this lack of supplies would lead to mutiny by the army.

Wives and relatives of the enlisted would alleviate some of this suffering by providing services that they needed desperately, including nursing and laundry. Some of these people were called the Regimental Camp Followers and also helped to increase morale of the army.

Supply Restoration

While Washington petitioned repeatedly for supplies and relief, the Continental Congress was not able to provide these needed items and the army suffered.

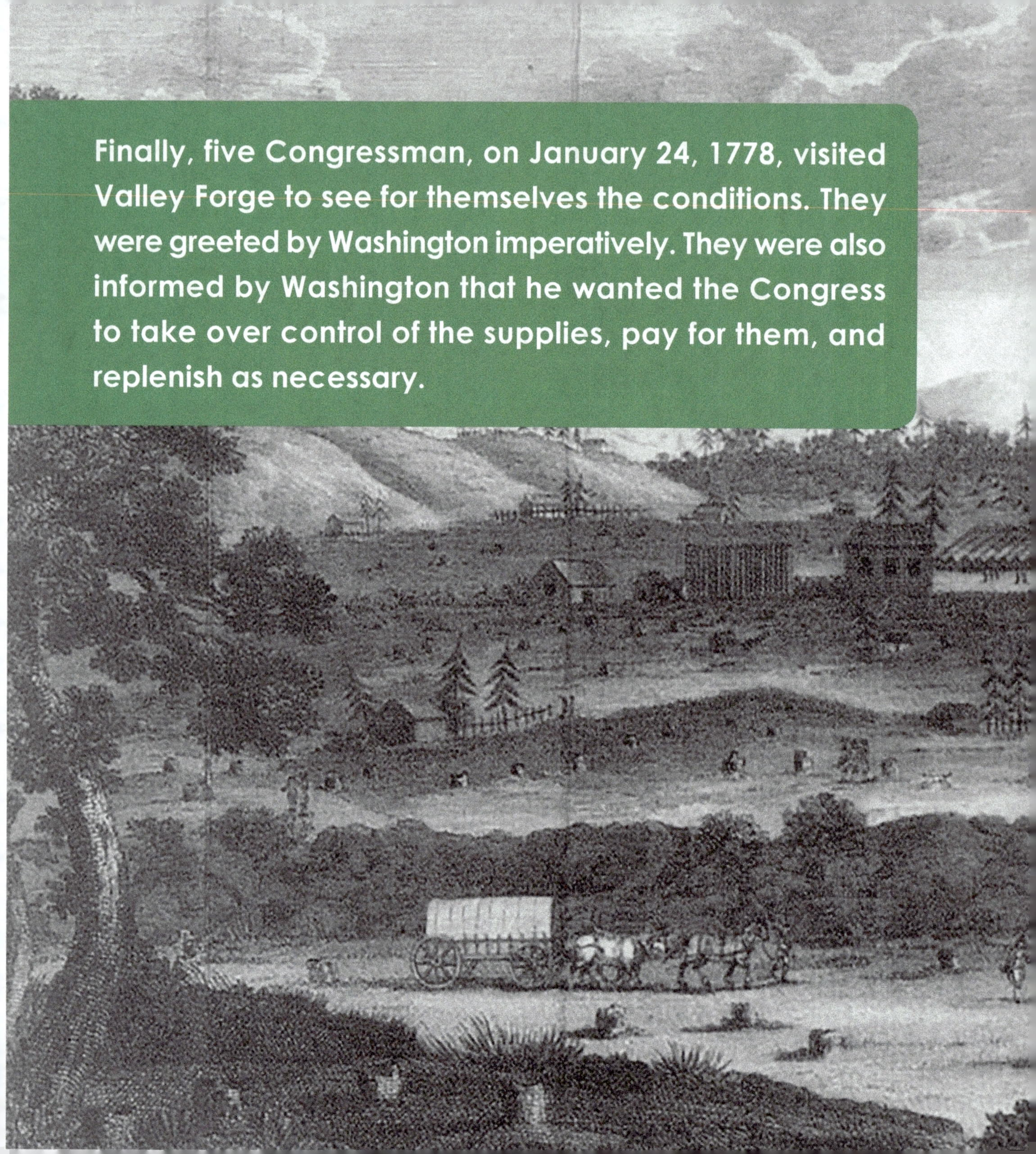

Finally, five Congressman, on January 24, 1778, visited Valley Forge to see for themselves the conditions. They were greeted by Washington imperatively. They were also informed by Washington that he wanted the Congress to take over control of the supplies, pay for them, and replenish as necessary.

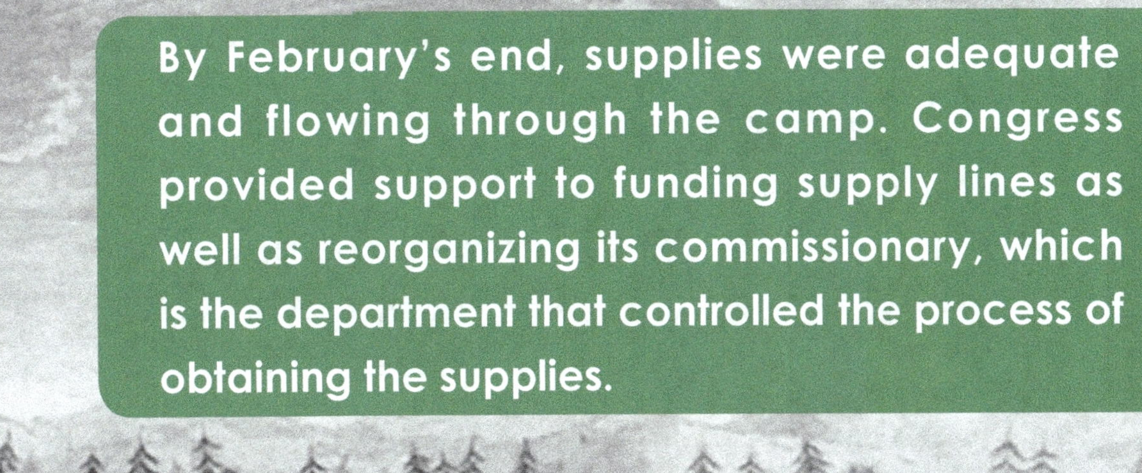
By February's end, supplies were adequate and flowing through the camp. Congress provided support to funding supply lines as well as reorganizing its commissionary, which is the department that controlled the process of obtaining the supplies.

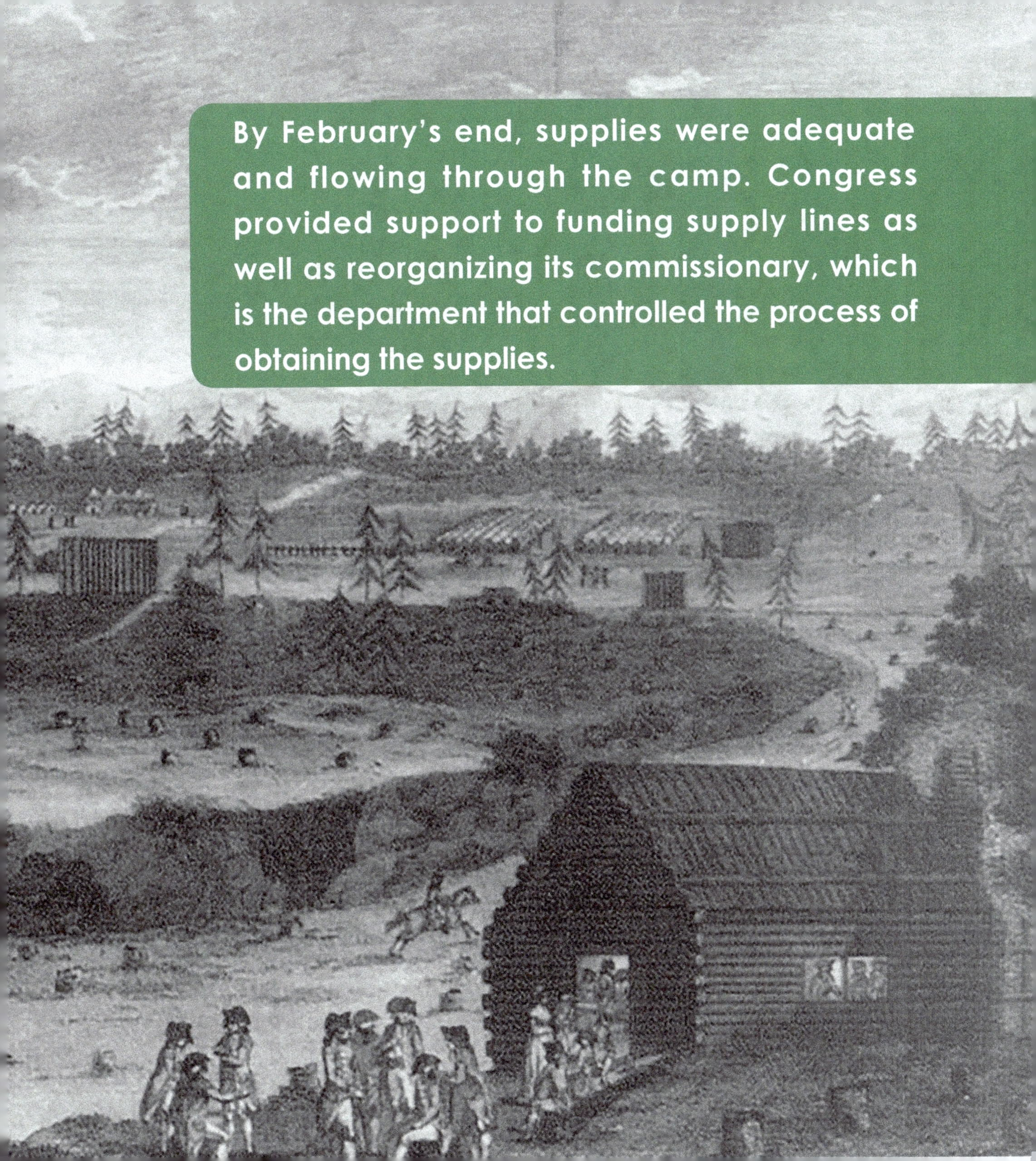

With the morale, discipline, and efficiency increasing, it became just as fundamental to the well-being of the army as the food supply to have proper training. It had become a problem during the battle due to the difficulty with training using the variety of manuals, which made battle coordination difficult. The soldiers were not training uniformly. Steuben then overtook the training program and was able to improve their battle skills tremendously.

Women and children

Martha Washington, George Washington's wife, arrived February 10, 1778. She paid visits to soldiers in the hospital and in their huts. She also started a sewing circle, a group of women that crafted, knitted, and patched socks of the soldiers, their shirts, and their trousers.

The Camp Followers were a group of wives, mothers, sisters and children of soldiers. These followers would often serve as laundresses, mending and cleaning their uniforms.

Washington knew that his men would pass away quick from disease if their uniform was threadbare and dirty. The children and women also gave them emotional support, encouraging them to stay at camp and remain training during the winter. If the Camp Followers completed their work they would receive 1/2 a days pay and half the rations of a soldier. Children received quarter rations although this is not documented.

Aftermath

The Continental Army discovered France was going to assist their cause by sending monetary and military donations to the army. After General Gate's army won the Battle of Saratoga, they had signed an alliance on February 6, 1778 with thirteen colonies. A celebration was organized at Valley Forge on May 6. 1778.

The army continued to shout "Long live France! Long live the friendly powers! Long live the American States!". Soldiers then performed drill formations and fired salutes from their cannons and muskets. At the end of this celebration, each person received some rum as a reward.

Word soon spread about the departure of the British which brought frantic activity to the Continental Army. On June 19, 1778, they then marched from Valley Forge, six months from when they arrived.

They then pursued the British, who were on their way to New York City. On June 28, 1778, the Battle of Monmouth took place which turned into an indecisive victory, even though Congress treated it like an American Victory once the British retreated. This demonstrated that the colonists could now withstand a British army after the training under von Steuben, which boosted morale and improved Washington's reputation as Commander in Chief.

The winter at Valley Forge instilled into these soldiers a will to triumph, endure, and persevere obstacles and brought independence to the United States. Washington acknowledged the perseverance acquired by these soldiers was what made the Army come together stronger and win the war.

However, there were many resignations of the officers. It was among the trials and struggles that Washington created a strong bond of friendship with the younger Lafayette.

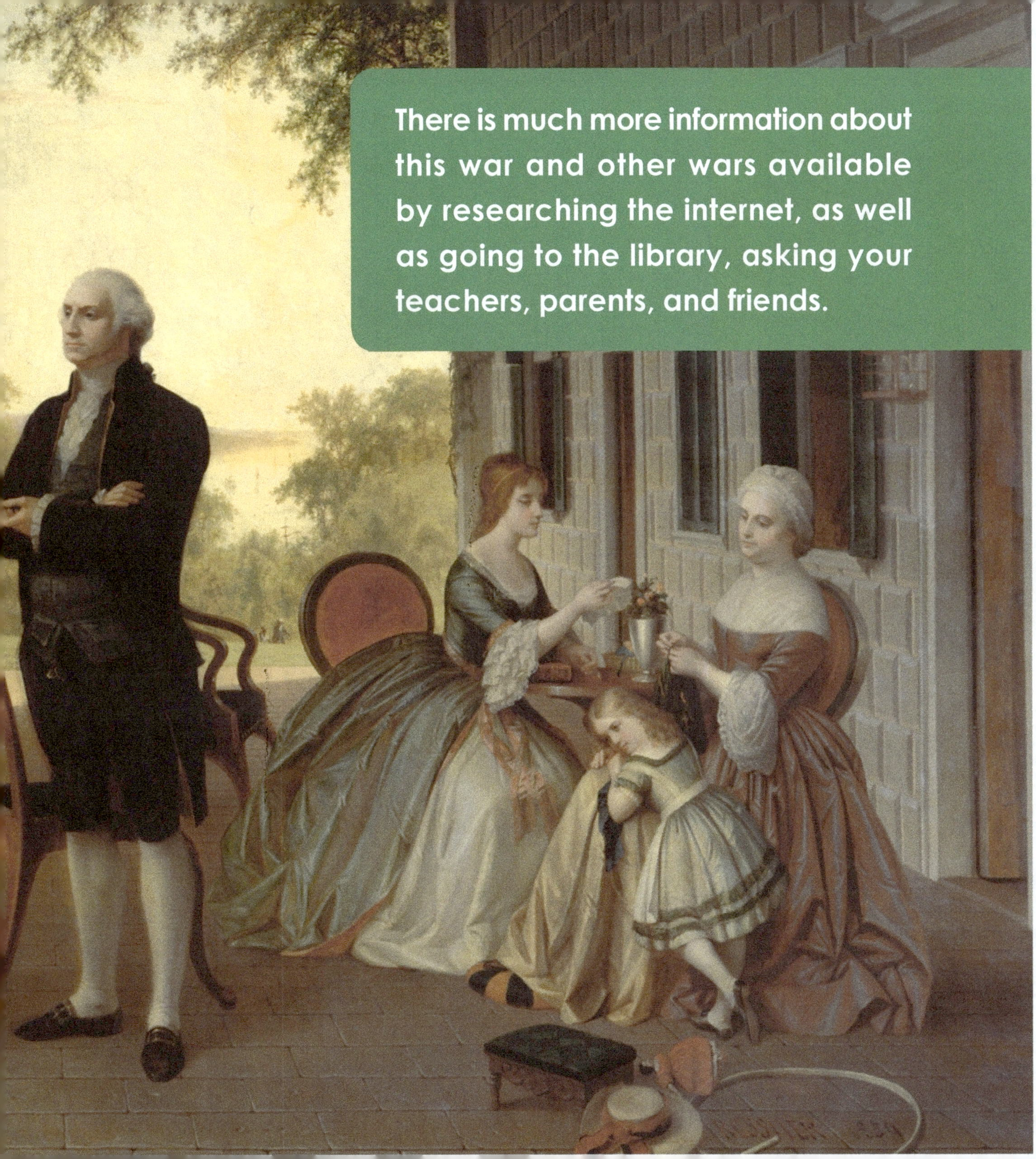

There is much more information about this war and other wars available by researching the internet, as well as going to the library, asking your teachers, parents, and friends.

Visit
BABY PROFESSOR
EDUCATION KIDS
www.BabyProfessorBooks.com
to download Free Baby Professor eBooks
and view our catalog of new and exciting
Children's Books